W9-AMV-570

by Tim O'Brien

CCC PUBLICATIONS

Published by

CCC Publications
1111 Rancho Conejo Blvd.
Suites 411 & 412
Newbury Park, CA 91320

Manufactured in the United States of America

Cover ©1995 CCC Publications

Cover/Interior production by Oasis Graphics

ISBN: 0-918259-94-0

If your local U.S. bookstore is out of stock, copies
of this book may be obtained by mailing check or
money order for $4.99 per book (plus $2.50 to
cover postage and handling) to: CCC Publications;
111 Rancho Conejo Blvd.; Suites 411 & 412;
Newbury Park, CA 91320

Pre-publication Edition – 10/95

INTRODUCTION

What can one expect of a book entitled simply "**?**" ? Maybe, like that best selling book of questions, it's a vessel for delving into the depths of one's psyche; a menu of inquiries to test one's morality. But then, those things are usually written by people whose names end in Ph.D. (All that follows this author's name is often a faintly uttered "who"?)

Perhaps it's a book of trivia...delightful tidbits that consume much of our cerebral storage space; gray matter that may have been previously reserved for the cure for cancer or the meaning of life. Of course, I would never want to be a deterrent to modern medicine.

Or maybe it's not a question mark at all. Maybe it's an exclamation point with a bad case of osteoporosis. (You'd be surprised how many punctuation marks are calcium-deficient.)

Actually, "**?**" is one man's cumulation of befuddlements that he hopes will have your excessively slapped knees covered with contusions—and your sides in dire need of medical stitch work.

Then again, if these fun little conundrums don't make you guffaw— I hope at least they'll give you a bit of a grin.

ACKNOWLEDGEMENTS

Thanks to Mom and Dad, whose amalgam of DNA material (and upbringing) has given me the perfect balance of rationality and irreverence. To my grandfather who is more hip than a Dunkin Donuts parking lot full of plaid-clad X'ers. And to Mary Pat Cupertino and Jeff Ericksen, for their wit and insight in helping with this book. You guyz iz funny!

Thanks most of all to
Diana; Co-author/Proofreader/Therapist/
Consultant/ Personal Motivational Speaker/
Partner Extraordinaire/Goddess.

1

Do chickens think rubber humans are funny?

2

When it rains in the summer, do cotton fields shrink?

3

Do cannibals get hungry one hour after eating a Chinaman?

4

Why do you see pet dogs
wearing sweaters but you
never see a pet fish
in bathing trunks?

5

Could it be that we *all* suffer from narcolepsy, only for most of us it just happens to strike about the same time every night?

6

Do people who play the washboard think of it as playing an acoustic washing machine?

7

Was there a less successful version of Cliffs Notes called Cliffords Condensed Notations?

8

If you were to use your carphone for phone sex, should you call from the backseat?

9

Do Roman paramedics refer to IVs as "4s?"

10

Just *before* someone gets nervous, do they experience cocoons in their stomach?

11

Will playing a Satanic message
backwards turn
a teenager into a
heavy metal worshipper?

12

When presenting a new bulletin board, should the vendor first let you smell the cork?

13

If a fetus is exposed to cellular phone waves, might it be born umbilical cordless?

14

Does distressed leather come from very tense cows?

15

At the risk of sounding paranoid, why is that p at the beginning of the word "psycho" always so darn silent?

16

Is there a group, like Alcoholics Anonymous, for people who abuse acronyms? If so, what do they call it for short?

17

Isn't a rosary really nothing
but a religious abacus?

18

When you see a mime fighting those heavy winds, do you ever wonder why he doesn't just get back into his imaginary box?

19

Wouldn't it be fun to take the lights at a sports arena and hook them up to "The Clapper?"

20

If the #2 pencil is the most popular, why's it still #2?

21

Instead of talking to your plants, if you *yelled* at them would they still grow, but only to be troubled and insecure?

22

After eating, do amphibians have to wait one hour before getting *out* of the water?

23

As a child, did Gandhi need
a pacifier?

24

Is it illegal to run into a crowded fire and yell "Theater!?"

25

If your eyes are the windows to your soul, does that make your eyebrows the valances?

When your pet bird sees you reading the newspaper, does he wonder why you're just sitting there, staring at carpeting?

27

Isn't it ironic that, in this world, there exists both escalators *and* Stairmasters?

28

As a rule, do the guys who paint the inside walls of art museums suffer from severe inferiority complexes?

29

Could an adult ever die of *delayed* infant death syndrome?

30

If you didn't want people to know you were an optimist, would you look at the world through rose-colored contact lenses?

31

Has there ever been a dueling banjos to the death?

32

Do indecisive squids discharge erasable ink?

33

If your furniture had a wild kegger party, how could you tell when the lamps were getting out of control?

34

Can you get high from sniffing a dead horse?

35

If someone tried to commit suicide by overdosing, but took a bottle of placebos instead; would he only *think* he were dead?

36

Does the average bird think *tree* houses are "birdhouses of the rich and famous?"

37

How does a shelf salesman keep his store from looking empty?

38

If a celebrity's signature is worth, say $1,000, and he wanted to purchase something that happened to cost $1,000, could he just sign a personal check made out for zero dollars?

39

Instead of "the backstroke" why not call it "making water angels?"

<u>4</u>0

If white wine goes with fish,
do white grapes go with sushi?

41

Does the French militia use
Dijon mustard gas?

42

Does a blind tourist use a sightseeing eye dog?

43

If someone took a blood test and found out theirs was B-, if they studied real hard, could they move up to type A?

44

When a palm reader reads a child's palm, does it rhyme?

45

Is it possible that "Memorex" is the name of an all-mime band and those tapes aren't blank after all?

46

Do clowns wear really big *socks*?

47

Why, when you're "making a living" you're barely making enough to survive, but when you're "making a killing" you're making enough to *really* live?

48

Would a Jewish Ninja use a throwing star of David?

49

Is there another word for
"synonym?"

50

Next time you lose your keys why not induce a near death experience so that, when your life passes before your eyes, you can see where you left them?

51

Technically, are women's birthday suits considered double-breasted?

52

How do you suggest that they
ought to fix the hole
in the bottom of a
suggestion box?

53

After dining on toothpicks, do termites clean their teeth with pieces of spinach?

54

If someone has a glass eye, does it fog up when they take a hot shower?

55

Could someone ever get addicted to counseling? If so, how could you treat them?

56

Should a mute get scolded for talking with his *hands* full?

57

Let's say you have half a glass of arsenic? *Now* how would the optimist see it?

58

If oysters are aphrodisiacs, does that mean oysters *themselves* are always horny?

59

Why was Evelyn Woods in
such a big hurry?

60

If there was a *bisexual* pride parade, would it go both ways?

61

Could it be that all those trick-or-treaters wearing sheets aren't going as ghosts, but actually as mattresses?

62

How do you let someone know you just painted a "Wet Paint" sign?

63

If someone is graduating from modeling school but trips going down the runway to get their diploma, would they still graduate?

64

Do used car salesmen prefer polyester candy to cotton candy?

65

Would you really hang a stickman? Wouldn't you just starve him instead because that wouldn't take very long, what with him being a stick already?

66

When two funeral processions meet at an intersection, how do they decide who has the right of way?

67

Why did they make the word
"dyslexia" so darn hard
to read?

68

Let's say you trip on a stalagmite and it embeds into your stomach, and then you tumble onto your back in pain. Since it's now directed downward, would it be classified as a *stalactite*?

69

Do police sketch artists start
out as those guys who outline
dead bodies?

70

Why don't they just make food
stamps edible?

71

Before receiving his Ph.D., was Doc's name an adjective like Dopey and all the other dwarfs? For example...."Smarty?"

72

Is there such a thing as dried
fruit flies?

73

To complement the vest, why not some nice bullet-proof slacks?

74

Back in the days of fur trading, did they use rat pelts for small change?

75

Wouldn't it be amusingly ironic if, during a war, the enemy accidentally bombed a clay pigeon factory?

76

Should crematoriums give discounts for burn victims?

77

Are rodeo clowns really just bad clowns who aren't very funny, or rodeo guys with a really good sense of humor?

78

If a mute swears, does his mother make him wash his *hands* with soap?

What would have happened
had Dr. Rorschach ever got his
inkblots mixed up with
Dr. Pap's smears?

80

When a taxidermist stuffs *his* Thanksgiving turkey, does he leave the head and feathers on?

81

Are circus midgets who get shot out of cannons called "human BB's?"

82

What does it mean if someone finds their funny bone only slightly amusing? Is it from lacking a sense of humor, or a deficiency of calcium?

83

When clumsy buzz saw operators go to sporting events, after a big play do they give each other the "high four?"

84

Should animal shampoo be tested on humans?

85

If a near-sighted Cyclops had
to wear a monocle, would
bully Cyclops yell
"hey Two Eyes?"

86

Is an empty beanbag chair still
a chair, or just a giant beanbag?

87

Why don't they call
moustaches "mouthbrows"?

88

How many of us may actually be giants who just happen to suffer from dwarfism?

89

If someone has a mid-life crisis
while playing hide & seek,
does he automatically
lose because he can't find
himself?

90

Could it be that boulders are really just statues of big rocks?

91

Since artificial insemination is self-imposed, should we say "the rabbit committed suicide?"

92

If a person thinks marathons are superior to sprints....is that racism?

93

If someone with multiple personalities threatens to kill himself, is it considered a hostage situation?

94

If a case of the clap spreads, is
it then considered a case of the
applause?

<u>95</u>

Is a mute with the shakes
considered a stutterer?

96

Like some advocates who wea
red ribbons, do carpal tunnel
syndrome advocates
wear typewriter ribbons?

97

f the pope is infallible, how do
you explain his choice of hats?

98

Isn't it a bit unnerving that doctors call what they do "practice"?

99

Is there such a thing as a nudist ant colony?

100

Could it be that so many deer get hit on the interstates because they're simply obeying the posted deer-crossing signs?

101

Did the early settlers ever go on camping trips?

102

What happens if a blind person is afraid of the dark?

103

Okay, so sticks and stones may break your bones but names can never hurt you. What if someone carved a name in stone and then *threw* it at you?

104

Can anyone do a decent Rich Little impersonation?

105

What do little birdies see when *they* get knocked unconscious?

106

Why don't they make cookies with powdered milk so all you'd have to do is dunk them in water?

107

Whose cruel idea was it for the word "lisp" to have an "S" in it?

108

If a Catholic Eskimo were to meet the pope, would he rub his nose on the pope's ring?

109

Why aren't there prescription windshields?

110

If you cut a blind man's cane in half while he's sleeping, would he think he grew three feet overnight?

111

Are ham radios available in the honey-cured variety?

112

Did Oedipus call his obsession
with his mother a
"Me Complex"?

113

Where do forest rangers go to "get away from it all"?

114

Wouldn't it be smarter to label "top secret" documents something less conspicuous like "trivial information which would only bore you to tears"?

115

Could Jesus turn seltzer water into wine spritzers?

116

How can there be self-help *groups*?

117

How do you throw away a garbage can?

118

Why is a dot when it's by itself just a dot, but when it's with other dots it suddenly becomes a polka dot?

119

Has an elephant ever been diagnosed with humanitis?

120

Instead of wasting time hunting *and* cooking, why don't hunters just use blowtorches?

121

Did old Roman scholars ever have cardigan parties?

122

Can you tell how old a pirate is by cutting off his peg and counting the rings?

123

To help improve their scores, why don't more people bowl during earthquakes?

124

What makes cheese so confidential that we actually need cheese shredders?

125

Why don't more masked robbers hold up ski lodges?

126

If a farmer forgets to shut one of his barn doors, should you tell him his zipper's open?

127

When a guillotine executioner takes a snapshot of someone, does he, out of habit, cut off the head?

128

What does it mean if you break a mirror with a rabbit's foot?

129

Instead of having to lick your fingers to turn *each* page of a book, why not just dunk one corner of the book in a bowl of water?

130

Is it possible to have
extra sensory *depth* perception?
If so, does it mean you know
exactly how close things will
be before ever approaching
them?

131

Do you feed a boogie fever?

132

Let's say someone, on a whim, had the entire history of Western Civilization tattooed on their arm and then, years later, found out they had to take a test on Western Civilization. Would that be cheating?

133

Do horses ever get together for a game of "penny loafers"?

134

Do onanists like to play strip solitaire?

135

How can you tell if a cartoon family's picture is a photo or a portrait?

136

How, if they can't see their reflections, do vampires always get their hair so nice?

137

What do you say to someone who asks if the gift you bought them is bigger or smaller than a breadbox, when the gift actually *is* a breadbox?

138

Do Scottish terriers get Scotch tapeworms?

139

When Indians have respiratory problems, are they put into oxygen *tepees*?

140

How many people thought of the Post-it Note before it was invented but just didn't have anything to jot it down on?

141

In juvenile court, instead of "mistrials," do they have "do-overs"?

142

Come tax time, can race car drivers deduct speeding tickets?

143

Why isn't there mouse-
flavored cat food?

144

During marching band competitions, for intermission shouldn't they have a quick game of football?

145

When vultures are on their deathbed, are they ever tempted to eat themselves?

146

Do Canadian cowboys wear 3.785 dekaliter hats?

147

Was the pole vault accidentally discovered by a clumsy javelin thrower?

148

How do you display
an easel?

149

Why do they report power
outages on TV?

150

Do people who make scale models of buildings start with microscopic scale models of the scale models?

151

Considering its total lack of tactile sensation, why would a toaster need a cozy?

152

While natural disasters are nothing to laugh at, wouldn't i be kind of funny if a tornado were to hit a wind chime factory?

153

Why are builders afraid
to have a 13th floor but book
publishers aren't
afraid to have a
Chapter 11?

154

When sign makers go on strike, do they carry *blank* picket signs?

155

Do those poker-playing dogs own paintings of humans playing fetch?

156

Can you return a
boomerang?

157

f a Raindancer were to do the
twist, would he create
waterspouts?

158

Is there a denture fairy who, instead of real coins, leaves slugs?

159

Which came first, the chicken salad sandwich or the egg salad sandwich?

160

Do bleached blondes just *pretend* to have more fun?

161

When you open a new bag of cotton balls, is the top one meant to be thrown away?

162

If you wanted to sell a new, unused price tag, where would you put the price?

163

Is a taxi's occupancy limit higher for clowns?

164

In a seven layer salad, do the bacon bits count as a layer, and if so, is that really fair?

165

Does the person in charge of taking a sheep farm's inventory often fall asleep on the job?

166

If oysters wore jewelry, would they make necklaces out of kidney stones?

167

Considering the overwhelming number of lint traps, and how the lint is carelessly thrown away...why aren't there more *lint* rights activists?

168

Why do people always remember where they were when someone famous was killed? Do they feel perhaps they'll need an alibi?

169

If you were to accidentally eat plastic fruit, when you threw up, would it be that wacky fake vomit?

TITLES BY CCC PUBLICATIONS

Retail $4.99

"?"

POSITIVELY PREGNANT
SIGNS YOUR SEX LIFE IS DEAD
WHY MEN DON'T HAVE A CLUE
40 AND HOLDING YOUR OWN
CAN SEX IMPROVE YOUR GOLF?
THE COMPLETE BOOGER BOOK
THINGS YOU CAN DO WITH A USELESS MAN
FLYING FUNNIES
MARITAL BLISS & OXYMORONS
THE VERY VERY SEXY ADULT DOT-TO-DOT BOOK
THE DEFINITIVE FART BOOK
THE COMPLETE WIMP'S GUIDE TO SEX
THE CAT OWNER'S SHAPE UP MANUAL
PMS CRAZED: TOUCH ME AND I'LL KILL YOU!
RETIRED: LET THE GAMES BEGIN
MALE BASHING: WOMEN'S FAVORITE PASTIME
THE OFFICE FROM HELL
FOOD & SEX
FITNESS FANATICS
YOUNGER MEN ARE BETTER THAN RETIN-A
BUT OSSIFER, IT'S NOT MY FAULT

Retail $5.95

LITTLE INSTRUCTION BOOK OF THE RICH & FAMOUS
GETTING EVEN WITH THE ANSWERING MACHINE
ARE YOU A SPORTS NUT?
MEN ARE PIGS / WOMEN ARE BITCHES
50 WAYS TO HUSTLE YOUR FRIENDS ($5.99)
HORMONES FROM HELL
HUSBANDS FROM HELL
KILLER BRAS & Other Hazards Of The 50's
IT'S BETTER TO BE OVER THE HILL THAN UNDER IT
HOW TO REALLY PARTY!!!
WORK SUCKS!
THE PEOPLE WATCHER'S FIRLD GUIDE
THE UNOFFICIAL WOMEN'S DIVORCE GUIDE
THE ABSOLUTE LAST CHANCE DIET BOOK
FOR MEN ONLY (How To Survive Marriage)
THE UGLY TRUTH ABOUT MEN
NEVER A DULL CARD
RED HOT MONOGAMY
  (In Just 60 Seconds A Day) ($6.95)

NO HANG-UPS – CASSETTES Retail $4.98

Vol. I: GENERAL MESSAGES (Female)
Vol. I: GENERAL MESSAGES (Male)
Vol. II: BUSINESS MESSAGES (Female)
Vol. II: BUSINESS MESSAGES (Male)
Vol. III: 'R' RATED MESSAGES (Female)
Vol. III: 'R' RATED MESSAGES (Male)
Vol. IV: SOUND EFFECTS ONLY
Vol. V: CELEBRI-TEASE

Retail $4.95

1001 WAYS TO PROCRASTINATE
THE WORLD'S GREATEST PUT-DOWN LINES
HORMONES FROM HELL II
SHARING THE ROAD WITH IDIOTS
THE GREATEST ANSWERING MACHINE MESSAGES
   OF ALL TIME
WHAT DO WE DO NOW?? (A Guide For New Parents)
HOW TO TALK YOU WAY OUT OF A TRAFFIC TICKET
THE BOTTOM HALF (How To Spot Incompetent
   Professionals)
LIFE'S MOST EMBARRASSING MOMENTS
HOW TO ENTERTAIN PEOPLE YOU HATE
YOUR GUIDE TO CORPORATE SURVIVAL
THE SUPERIOR PERSON'S GUIDE TO EVERYDAY
   IRRITATIONS
GIFTING RIGHT

Retail $3.95

YOU KNOW YOU'RE AN OLD FART WHEN...
NO HANG-UPS
NO HANG-UPS II
NO HANG-UPS III
HOW TO SUCCEED IN SINGLES BARS
HOW TO GET EVEN WITH YOUR EXES
TOTALLY OUTRAGEOUS BUMPER-SNICKERS ($2.95